Philosophy
of
Spiritualism

Minister Barry Oates
Minister David Hopkins
Officiant Carole Austin

Dedicated to the memory of
Emma Hardinge Britten
without whose inspiration this book
would not have been possible.

ISBN 978 901958 14 0

Introduction

When the phrase 'Philosophy of Spiritualism' is used in this and allied publications, it indicates the religious philosophy based on the Seven Principles. The ideas encompassed in these principles were given over a period of years in the latter part of the nineteenth century and laid down in their present form in the Articles of Association of a corporate body established in 1901 with the title 'Spiritualists' National Union' (SNU). The philosophy is that which has been created by and through those who have been involved with the SNU.

The Seven Principles are the foundation of the religious philosophy of Spiritualism. When the Principles were laid down over a hundred years ago, they were framed in the words and terms of their time. The limitations of language, together with the changes in meaning and interpretation that have taken place over time, render argument over words of little value. Our understanding today, for example, of the term 'God' has grown from how God was seen thousands, hundreds or even tens of years ago to the views that are held now in the 21st century. As we develop we trust that our understanding will grow.

Spiritualists do not claim to have complete knowledge of spiritual matters. Spiritualist philosophy draws on the wisdom of mankind that has accumulated over time and also seeks to incorporate current understanding. For that reason, the interpretation of the Seven Principles set down in this document is not to be seen as absolute or definitive. As more is learned, we will understand more and be better equipped to pass on the wisdom of Spirit.

The intention of this book is to provide clarity and guidance on the philosophy of Spiritualism. Whilst it is considered desirable to reach a consensus of ideas within Spiritualism, the rights and opinions of the individual will always be accepted and valued. There is no monopoly on truth or the understanding of truth, but to have unity of purpose a common understanding is needed. In this imperfect existence we cannot fully comprehend perfection. We can only strive to achieve closer alignment with it.

It should be understood that the equality and complete integration of male and female qualities is inherent in all wording used in the text of this book and the generally accepted linguistic use of the masculine gender refers to both male and female persons. The terminology employed is intended to imply a wholeness of life, not a fragmentation.

This explanation of the Seven Principles presents a summary of understanding at the time of publication. If it is helpful to the reader, then it is a valuable tool in his ongoing study of Spiritualism. If it is not, then it is hoped that sometime and somewhere he will find what he is seeking.

In writing this book the authors gratefully acknowledge the support and inspiration given by many others who reside both in this world and the next.

Minister Barry Oates
Minister David Hopkins
Officiant Carole Austin

Philosophy and Ethics Committee,
The Spiritualists' National Union

The Seven Principles of Spiritualism

1 The Fatherhood of God

2 The Brotherhood of Man

3 The Communion of Spirits and
   the Ministry of Angels

4 The Continuous Existence of
   the Human Soul

5 Personal Responsibility

6 Compensation and Retribution Hereafter
   for all the Good and Evil Deeds
   done on Earth

7 Eternal Progress Open to Every
   Human Soul

First Principle

The Fatherhood of God

Nature of God

It is impossible for man to understand fully the true nature of God because the concept of such a Being transcends the limited mental faculties of humankind. What is infinite cannot be comprehended by finite minds.

Spiritualism teaches that God, often referred to as 'The Great Spirit' or 'The Great White Spirit', is All That Is, the Ultimate Reality and the Totality of Being, outside of Which nothing can exist. God is the Eternal Source of all life, the Divine Creative Energy, Which flows through the universe and incessantly animates, sustains and nurtures all creation. God is the Supreme Mind, the Great Cosmic Consciousness, the Directive Intelligence behind the universe, an eternal, all-powerful, all-knowing, all-pervading Being Who manifests in all things and of Whom all things are part.

God is the Universal Spirit, the Divine Parent, Who dwells in everything, infinite in essence, unlimited in power and perfect in attribute, forever seeking expression in an infinite variety of forms. God is the Supreme Mind, the perfect embodiment of love, joy, knowledge, wisdom, justice, truth and power, Who manifests through the operation of the natural laws of the universe. There can be no suspension of these laws, and apparent miracles are, in reality, the operation of laws at present not fully understood by mankind.

God is Love and Light. God's love is the sustaining force of the universe and is the manifesting source of all creation. Man is part of God but not the whole of God. God exists in all the myriad forms of life throughout the universe at one and the same time. We are all at one with our Creator and with each other. Although on a material level we experience ourselves as being separate from God, each having our own unique individuality, we are in reality linked to God and each other and can never be separated. We stand in relationship to God as a drop of water to the ocean.

God is conscious of the whole of creation and is eternally aware of its needs. Although God is perfection, He is still expanding His experience through the evolution of His creation.

9

God cannot be identified in personal terms because He is not an individual, a personal being or a deified man with human imperfections, weaknesses and emotions. He is beyond form, since this would be a limitation on the expression of the Divine Spirit, but He comes into form and manifests Himself through all of His creations as individualised expressions of the whole. God is neither male nor female, combining both the masculine and feminine principles in one Being, and thus is better thought of as Father-Mother God.

Creation of the Universe

God is so utterly transcendent in nature to man that the latter can never have any definite conception of the Divine Being. However, as the Divine Spirit has been responsible for the creation and sustenance of the universe, man can form some conception of His ways of working and therefore of His nature by studying the universe and the laws which operate in it.

James F. Malcolm

The creation of the universe and the beginning of time are at present beyond man's understanding, but it may be hypothesised that aeons ago God existed in an awareness only of Himself and that there was nothing other than God. In time He manifested in separate form and this synthesis of God's mind led to the creation of the complex whole which we know as the physical universe. Particles of life arose which eventually developed into the fullness of the natural world we know today. Thus, from a realm of perfection there arose a relative world with opposites, which has God as the Directing Mind and Divine Planner behind all that is.

Science demonstrates that our planet is but a speck in a solar system that is part of a galaxy and also that there are uncountable numbers of other galaxies. There may be millions of planets in the universe and we are like one grain of sand on a vast seashore, but this is not some haphazard scattering of grit, for there is order, planning and balance. There is constant expansion and constant creation, but it is not a case of the same amount of matter being spread ever more thinly. The universe is expanding at a phenomenal rate and there

10

are galaxies moving away from us so rapidly that we can never see them. Yet this energy, power, speed and distance are subject to natural laws. Who can question that there is something in control? It would be illogical to think otherwise.

Even on our small globe we see the distance to our sun, the arrangement of night and day, gravity, the tidal effects of the moon and the other physical features of our environment which together produce exactly the right conditions for human life. Science has demonstrated distances and times in the universe that are beyond our understanding. Even with the speed of light it has taken two thousand million years for the light of distant stars to reach us. We see them through powerful telescopes as they were two thousand million years ago. How can we comprehend such immense distances of time?

We do not know what constitutes life. We see it manifesting in myriad forms but cannot define it. Observation leads to the conclusion that there is a vital energy which creates and maintains all that is, but there is also a spiritual dimension that extends beyond the physical universe. We do not know exactly how the physical and spiritual intermingle, but there are things we accept but cannot yet explain. Who has not been sustained by meditation, prayer or music, when the mind has attuned with higher spiritual energy? For many, the spiritual is the more important, while the physical allows the opportunity for experiences that help personal development.

Creation, both physical and spiritual, is not from a void but is of the Great Spirit. We cannot be where God is not.

Creation and Evolution of Life

God created and constructed the universe and all that is, has ever been and ever will be. This creation encompasses everything that is presently known to mankind and possibly much that is yet to be discovered. It is believed that many celestial bodies lack the specific conditions for promotion of life as we know it, while the planet on which we live is fortunate in having the right combination of life-giving and life-sustaining components for the propagation of living organisms. God in His wisdom has provided our home planet with an environment through which He can express Himself in living things, mankind being but one of the multitudinous forms of animate life. The totality of plant and animal creation – the living, pulsating body of life – is wonderful and beautiful, each species forming part of the whole. Man is only a speck in the firmament of this creation but nevertheless has been brought into existence to move through the human experience of life.

Of the many forms of life on Earth, man appears to be the most intellectually advanced in terms of ingenuity and inventiveness and has developed highly sophisticated thought processes that enable him to mould and manipulate his environment. It would appear that there is a Divine Plan behind the evolution of Homo sapiens which has enabled man to develop into the thinking, social, creative and spiritual being that exists today. The human species has been blessed with an intellect that is capable of dealing not only with the practicalities of existence but also with the exploration of the mystical and spiritual aspects of being.

We must individually make the most of what has been given to us, whether we aspire to the highest or the lowest, the best or the worst. Each of us has been given the means by which to express himself as a spiritual being. We are neither good nor bad, we just are. Mankind is part of God's perfect creation and any imperfection in humankind arises from its reaction to physical life and failure to live in accordance with Universal Law. God is part of humanity and humanity is part of God; there are no divisions other than those for which mankind itself is responsible.

Ultimately there is but one Being that manifests in all forms and aspects of life. God is in the highest sense the Father-Mother, Creator of All, with the whole of mankind being part of His family. God creates the conditions that allow the individual to thrive as a spiritual being. He does not rule, He simply creates. Creation produces existence, whilst genetic law perpetuates that existence. The process of creation is continuous and never complete. What exists now is only part of the story that God wishes to write. Evolutionary development will alter what is known today and living things will change as God continues to expand Himself. We do not know where life will eventually lead as creation and evolution move forward. Life as we know it will progress in a way that is above and beyond what mere human beings can comprehend with their limited understanding.

As we contemplate the many wonders of life on Earth, it never fails to fill us with admiration and exhilaration that God has been able to express Himself in so many forms of life. The scale of His ingenuity and inventiveness is breathtaking and we are privileged to enjoy the beauties and wonders of the natural world and be part of the entire, sustaining and supportive cycle of life. Every living species has its own place and purpose and has evolved in accordance with the governing laws of nature. The life-force that drives and directs all living things is designed to ensure continuity and evolutionary progress. Creation and evolution are part of God's Divine Plan, which ensures that all of life is perfectly balanced within Universal Law. As we contemplate the magnificence of the world around us, we give thanks for our own lives and the lives of others and rejoice in being part of the whole of creation.

Relationship Between God and Man

The wording of the First Principle is 'The Fatherhood of God'. The word 'father' indicates that man has come from, or been created by, God and so is seen as a part of God. However, God has created much more than life expressed through man. Whatever exists, wherever it may be, is part of God. God is more than the totality of all the parts. As a writer creates characters within a book, yet still remains capable of writing other characters and is also more than the sum of his characters, so does God encompass all that He has created. He has the ability to create and develop life and is more than the total of that which has been, or ever will be, created.

As earthly parents endeavour to nurture their children, so we are maintained and sustained by God. If we choose not to distribute fairly the abundance that has been provided, the responsibility lies with us, not with God. Like a good parent, He provides far more than material succour. Our innate spiritual natures are also nurtured by His outpouring of knowledge, wisdom, truth and love. It is our responsibility to accept, understand and aspire to those concepts for our benefit.

Each of us is an aspect of God. Ultimately, there is only one single Being Who manifests in every form of existence throughout the universe. The Creator and the created are indivisible, for there can never be a time when the created can be separated from the Creator. Though the links may sometimes seem hidden, they are never broken. We may at times be less aware of God's influence than at others but, as Ultimate and Eternal Love, God will never, whatever the circumstances, turn away from what He has created. We never can be separated from God.

We conceive God in the highest sense as our 'parent', Father and Mother, and ourselves as part of one united family. There is a dependence upon, and interdependence with, God, yet man is nevertheless an individualisation of God's Spirit. Every being has its own imprint and uniqueness and has an essential part to play in the Plan of Life. The light of God is within us all, yet burning with different degrees of intensity.

Because of this indestructible link between Creator and created there is an ongoing revelation of wisdom and truth which can be accessed by everyone. As we become more aware of, and more in tune with, our spiritual nature, so do the quality and quantity of guidance increase. This is open for all to receive at the appropriate level, without need of intermediaries and being dependent only upon the individual stage of awareness. This wisdom is a natural development which allows us to access information from many sources and in many forms: through nature, intuition, dreams, inspiration and 'coincidence', as we come to understand and use our innate abilities.

We are all God in embryo, with the capability of reaching any and all our dreams and then surpassing them. The child is the repository of infinite possibility and we are all truly sons and daughters of God.

God's Purpose for Man

Having created a conscious, sentient being in man, God in His wisdom has given mankind the capability of thought, evaluation, contemplation and expansion of knowledge. The question has to be asked, 'Why?' Man has the ability to explore aspects of himself and his surroundings above and beyond his animal instincts and has been given a divine intelligence to use for better or for worse. He has the awareness of spirituality, which enables him to discover himself as a spiritual being and to walk the pathway of light and understanding as revealed by the will of God.

Man's purpose can be seen as twofold – to live a physical life with all its experiences, difficulties, joys and sorrows, whilst simultaneously exploring and expanding his spiritual self with its awareness of God and spirit. In having a dual role man is able to express himself both as a human being as part of the creation of animate life and also as a spiritual being as part of the creation of spirit life. The physical and the spiritual are indivisible in one human body, with lessons learnt by the flowing of one into the other. This relationship of body and spirit is designed to produce an awareness of God which will inspire and encourage spiritual development.

Man has the propensity to think, learn and educate himself. He also feels the need to expand his consciousness and seek knowledge for its own sake. An essential part of the human character is the need to push forward frontiers of knowledge, to expand boundaries and explore the unknown. Each time a new discovery is made, a new hypothesis tested, a new question asked, man is expressing part of God's purpose. Possessing a curiosity about the world, with answers to be sought and solutions to be found, leads to an expansion of awareness and a realisation that there is more to learn. Man rejoices in intellectual exercise and inventiveness because each new discovery reveals yet another aspect of the wonder of God.

That mankind sets itself the task of solving mysteries of a practical and intellectual nature is beyond dispute. Physical life in an earthly environment demands methods of survival that ensure continuation, sustenance and progression of the species. The human brain and mind that have developed to deal with practicality have nevertheless developed an aptitude also to think and feel spiritually. Whilst both abilities function side by side, together they form the whole being. Man comes to recognise that, whilst he operates in the physical world, he lives also in a spiritual environment.

The spiritual self is an essential part of human nature and as it is developed it creates a greater awareness of God. To love and be loved, to give and to receive, to serve and be served – such actions enrich the soul and give greater meaning to life, enabling the spirit to be more fully expressed during its earthly sojourn. The challenges and experiences of the physical plane and how they are dealt with present opportunities for spiritual evolution. The lesson for mankind is to understand that the physical vehicle, the body, encompasses the spirit, and it is the spirit that is the direct connection to God.

Natural Law directs everyone and everything. All creation has to conform to this divine directive because it is inescapable. Nothing can free itself from the obligations of Natural Law, no matter how high or low on the scale of life. Man may think he has free will through which to express himself but this free will can only be enacted within the boundaries of Natural Law. Man has always been, and always will be, part of the Great Divinity and by implementing Natural Law people will begin to understand their relationship to God. This Law, laid down by the Great Creator, is the foundation of natural justice – perfect law to create perfect function of the universe.

Spiritualism, through its teachings, encourages man to improve his quality of life by recognising and implementing Natural Law, thus expressing fully that part of the Great Spirit within himself. If the whole of humankind, individually and collectively, lived according to Natural Law in every thought, word and deed, then it would truly create a world of Natural Justice in which all could thrive. God's purpose for man would then be fulfilled.

Second Principle

The Brotherhood of Man

The Brotherhood of Man

The foundation of the religious philosophy of Spiritualism is the acceptance that there is a power we term 'God', the creative energy of the universe which has established, and thus links and binds, all that exists. Whilst the wording of the Second Principle of Spiritualism refers to what we call mankind, the ramifications go much wider than that and it can be inferred that the meaning includes other forms of life on Earth.

We shall, however, consider first the human race, which truly is a brotherhood. Scientific research has shown that mankind as we know it originated many thousands of years ago in Africa and that small families and groups migrated throughout the Earth, eventually evolving into the varied races and societies that exist today. Therefore all human beings, having originated from the same human family, share the attributes, feelings and emotions that define us as the species we are. We are aware that people live within different societies and cultures, but the main thread of human feeling and emotion nonetheless runs throughout. The ability to feel and think is common to the whole and what makes one part of mankind makes all. The bond that allows us to say we are truly brothers is the knowledge that, in essence, we are all the same and it is this unifying force that helps every human being to know and understand another. Thus we can draw a parallel between the existence of a spiritual brotherhood and the existence of a physical brotherhood.

Let us now consider man as mentioned in the Second Principle. Based upon the idea of God as Father, and accepting that humankind is thus the child of God, we can draw no conclusion other than that the Brotherhood of Man is a reality and not just an ideology or aspiration for the distant future.

In accepting brotherhood we should walk the spiritual journey of life together and promote love, tolerance and understanding among men. Having accepted the First Principle, The Fatherhood of God, it would seem a natural consequence to accept the Second Principle, The Brotherhood of Man. God loves each of us exactly as we are, with all our faults and imperfections. Why, then, should we not equally love our brothers and accept their faults and

19

imperfections, for we have before us the example of the Master who demonstrates the truth of absolute love?

A significant part of the lesson of human life is development of the qualities of tolerance and understanding – to test and endeavour to overcome negative responses by giving love in the face of adversity.

Spiritual progression is dependent upon our reaction to the problems we encounter in life, our relationships with others and our attitudes towards other forms of life. It could be said that differences exist to draw the attention of mankind to the fact that there is a lack of tolerance and love between people. Perhaps we are meant to recognise that we are not very tolerant and loving and need to be spurred into action to correct our ways.

We have to ask ourselves if it is possible in a world as diverse as the one in which we live to view the whole of humankind as brothers simply because it is the right thing to do. Can we love the whole of humanity to the point where we can truly call every man our brother? Love is the ideal, but perhaps kindness and compassion are more fitted to some situations where we find love difficult, or even impossible, to contemplate. Events and personalities sometimes give us cause to feel that love is out of the question and that too much is required of us. Kindness, tolerance and respect are good alternatives when we encounter such situations, but we should be aware that our goal is to overcome the feelings of antagonism or hostility that are aroused in us by the actions of others. We should strive to find the spiritual strength and awareness within ourselves to learn to love fully and without reservation.

This is, perhaps, one of the most difficult tasks we are set by the Divine Spirit – to love and understand others even though we disapprove of their behaviour or actions. We should reflect more carefully before making judgments because we may not be aware of all the facts surrounding people or situations. We may be unable to see matters clearly or accept an alternative point of view. Flexibility of thought and mind is essential. The more we are tested in the matter of love towards our brothers, the more we learn about ourselves. Human life is complex and the stresses and strains upon the individual are great. If we can find it within ourselves to move towards love and compassion in spite of difficult, or even dreadful, circumstances, then we shall truly have advanced our own understanding of the human condition.

The Brotherhood of Man should be based on love of humanity, together with tolerance of all those who experience the physical human existence. Tolerance is one of the most powerful aspects of life insofar as we do not need to love a fellow human being in order to respect the way he lives his life or the path he treads. We should remember that he also has the right to reach his goal and express his own understanding, even if it is different from our own.

The diversity of the world is exciting and challenging and presents us with all we require in order to progress physically as well as spiritually. If we accept that mankind comes from one source, God, then there must be a link between our brothers and ourselves. This relationship with the Divine Being means we are all endowed with a spiritual essence that is carried within us throughout our lives. It is learning to recognise this spiritual essence in others that is sometimes so difficult and problematical. We should accept, however, that what stretches us most also develops our personal awareness and moves us forward on the pathway of spiritual progression.

It is not easy to love everyone we encounter in life, and indeed would the purpose of life be served if we could? The Creator in His wisdom must have been aware of how we, as human beings, would react to the diversity of the world. What we consider to be negative aspects are not necessarily seen in the same way by others, yet we attempt to rectify situations because we consider it the right thing to do. We are inclined quite arbitrarily to impose on other people what we think is best for them, simply because we have made a personal judgment about their actions. We use our own standards when making an assessment of what we regard to be appropriate or right, without necessarily giving sufficient consideration to alternative points of view. We are inclined to make decisions about others and then conclude that their actions have not met our own criteria. We should, however, always allow for the fact that we may be wrong. The subtle complexities of human behaviour may be of greater magnitude than our meagre comprehension will allow and it is only the Divine Spirit Who is able to see the whole picture and pattern of life.

As long as humankind exists in this world, situations will present themselves that require the exercise of feeling, intellect and conscience. There will always be differences of habit, custom, opinion, gender, and background – things that help to create the rich variety and pattern of the world in which we live. Who would say that red is more important or better than green, that blue has more meaning than orange, that yellow has more value than violet? It is only by mixing colours in a multitude of combinations that the perfect picture can be painted in order to achieve the variation so essential in life.

Who would choose to experience life in a tone of grey rather than enjoy it in a thousand colours? If we lived in a world where we all looked, thought, talked, acted and reacted in exactly the same way, how long would it be before we cried out for something different? We need difference to challenge, to stimulate and to draw the best from each of us. Progress comes from those who both learn from, and teach, others. It is only by working together and sharing knowledge, hopes and aspirations that mankind can take forward the plan that has been set down for all that exists.

Having celebrated difference, it is also necessary to consider the bonds of similarity. We all have the capacity to love or loathe, laugh or cry, like or dislike. We all can share family feelings of loving and belonging, and we all have needs and desires. We also have the capacity to make friendships and feel joy for people who are fortunate, or sympathy for those who are less fortunate. These are natural human responses common to us all, both individually and collectively, in brotherhood.

In addition to natural human feelings we are blessed with an intellect that confers the ability to learn, teach and reason. We also have the ability to develop the higher mind and become aware of the spiritual self. These attributes help to create the special qualities of the human being, who is both an individual and an equal in brotherhood.

We are linked in a fraternal chain that extends across and around the Earth, reaching both backwards and forwards, encompassing all those who share this life and this world. We express brotherhood in loving and caring, in bringing hope and happiness to all, regardless of background and origin. Our love for our brothers should be inclusive of all peoples with no exceptions or omissions and should be a true reflection of the love we receive from our Father, the Great Spirit.

All forms of life stem from the same spiritual energy, the same power source, because man and every being are created as part of the Great Spirit. God has placed mankind at the helm of the vessel we share on the journey through life. It is therefore of the greatest importance that we accept the concept of caring and sharing for life in all its many and varied forms.

The Brotherhood of Man implies a love of humanity and life, but it also provides a clear understanding of the Creator and His intention for us. In striving to comprehend the diversity of the world and those who live in it we benefit not only ourselves but those who live in less fortunate conditions. In feeling compassion for people who experience distress and deprivation we are afforded the opportunity to acknowledge that "there but for the grace of God go I." If we are moved by the wretched plight of others we shall surely understand that a change of circumstance might easily bring us into an equally adverse situation.

We should therefore take instruction from such matters and help each other whenever and wherever possible. If we actively give help and consolation to people in need, we shall go a long way towards realising the true Brotherhood of Man, making an ideal a reality. God surely intends the complexities and difficulties of life to serve a purpose, even though we may not understand the complete purpose in our own lifetime. It may even be that we are not intended to know.

If, however, we try to put right in the most caring way possible something we consider to be wrong, we shall have offered ourselves in service no matter how small our contribution. Any action and thought given in love is for the greater good of all. We should balance our hope of creating a world that treats all men equally in a social, economic and political sense with the aspirations of others, which may differ from our own. We should try to understand ways of life and attitudes that are unlike those with which we are familiar. Some societies and cultures will inevitably be, and remain, different from our own and it is not for us to impose our ideals on them. If help is needed and asked for, then we should certainly try to respond. It is in the nature of mankind to prefer to be guided rather than led and for change to come about spontaneously from within, rather than be forced from outside.

It would be wrong of us to think that we are further ahead spiritually than others simply because we consider ourselves to be more advanced than some peoples or cultures: quite the contrary. It could be said that supposed less-developed societies are more spiritually aware and content with their lives than we are with our own. We tend to make judgments based on personal experiences and others equally have the right to do the same. True brotherhood requires that we seek to recognise what people really need, rather than what we think they need, and it may well be that they need nothing at all from us. If they feel we have nothing to offer, and also that they have nothing to learn, then we must wait for realisation to come to them in their own time. The lesson for us, however, is to be there when needed and never to impose our will unasked on others.

We must understand that the way some people choose to live their lives may not be our way. If their choice is wrong, ultimately they will see that they have impeded their spiritual progress. It is their lesson to learn, not ours to teach. This means that we must sometimes stand back and watch others harm themselves in order that they gain experience as they journey onward. The one thing that we can do, however, is to respond with loving kindness and give help whenever it is sought.

We see in life the best and the worst in humankind, a pattern repeated from historical times to the present day. Man's inhumanity to man can be seen at many levels, with prejudices as old as mankind itself causing unnecessary strife and destruction. War and conflict might have been prevented in many cases if tolerance, rather than force, had been the guiding principle.

Having considered the Brotherhood of Man, we have to acknowledge that we also share the planet on which we live with all other forms of life. These species should be embraced in brotherhood together with mankind because man is but one of the life-forms that exist on Earth. It is therefore incumbent upon us to give consideration and respect to all other living species. If we use any life-form to maintain or assist our physical life, then we must show compassion and respect for it. There may be times when for our own survival it may seem necessary to take life. If we are aware of our responsibilities to the life we take, if we have respect for its existence and its future progress, then we show an aspect of the love we in turn receive from the Great Spirit.

Scientific discovery frequently makes us aware of the existence of species of which we had no previous knowledge. What further discoveries can be expected as we continue to explore this small globe and then begin to explore the vastness of the universe? We can expect the unexpected.

The world, indeed the universe, is in a delicate and essential state of balance. We must maintain that balance at all costs. We stand at the pinnacle of life on Earth, having aptitude and knowledge beyond the abilities of most other forms of life whose environment we share. We are capable of exercising judgment, conscience and compassion in our ability to study, review, assess and decide on the course of action to take. We do not, or should not, act from instinct alone. Our God-given powers are such that we have a great measure of control over the direction of our own future and the future of the planet. With this knowledge and wisdom comes the necessity of balancing our rights with our responsibilities for those with whom we share the planet. Life on Earth takes innumerable forms and we are related to, and have a relationship with, each and every one of those forms.

We say that man is at or near the top of the chain of developed sentient beings on Earth. Such an assertion should be accompanied by recognition of a duty of care. If we consider our form of life to be pre-eminent in the world, this elevated position gives us a role different from, and possibly in many ways superior to, those of other species. Such a position may indicate our rights, but it also carries responsibilities. If we argue that other creatures have a subservient role, that some exist to serve mankind, then we should acknowledge also that we have a duty of care towards them. Our treatment of other species must, therefore, be in line with what we ourselves expect from the Creator: care, nourishment and protection. We must treat all forms of life with the respect that we would wish for ourselves.

Love, respect and understanding are indivisible. True Brotherhood will be built on these three aspects of human life because they form the foundation of a peaceful and compassionate existence which, when applied universally, will cure many of the ills that plague the world today. The diversity and excitement of life will remain, but it is our reaction to the challenge of living that will determine our worth as spiritual and physical beings. The beneficiaries of our success will be future generations who will understand the truth of Brotherhood and inherit a world of which we, and they, can be proud.

Third Principle

The Communion of Spirits
and
The Ministry of Angels

The Communion of Spirits

The gifts of mediumship are precious possessions and should be acquired only that Life and Service may be more fittingly offered to the Lord of Life. But if we have the true wisdom we shall realise that the most perfect gift is to live close to the Spirit World and to know and love its messengers so intimately that thought flows from soul to soul, not through the instrumentality of some friendly medium.

George F. Berry
The Seven-Pointed Star

The Third Principle of Spiritualism is an acknowledgement of the fact that communication with a world beyond our earthly world is possible. This principle confirms that Spiritualists know that life is a continuous process and that when we pass from this world to the next we will move onward to another sphere of existence. God in His wisdom allows communication between this world and the etheric realms and it must be said that this is not speculation by those who follow Spiritualism but the result of in-depth investigations over many years.

When considering the word 'communion' Spiritualists use the definition that means sharing, especially of thoughts, feelings and fellowship. Participation and sharing in common are important in Spiritualist philosophy because they encompass the communion we know to be an ongoing process without limitation between the physical world and the world of spirit.

In accepting the idea of sharing thoughts and feelings we can expand this to include the manner in which we share, that is, by the exchange of information. It is this aspect of communion which applies to communication between individual spirits, some of whom inhabit physical bodies and live in earthly conditions, and some of whom do not have physical form and inhabit the ethereal spheres of life. Just as we here on Earth vary in our levels of spiritual development, so also are those in the spirit world at different levels of spiritual evolution.

Just as spirit communicators are spiritual beings who do not have a physical body, so we on earth are spiritual beings who do have a physical body. Nevertheless, we and they are all spirit,

29

so the communion of spirits is a true union of spiritual beings. Through spiritual communion we receive spirit communication, which is the spiritual connection between our spirit helpers, our loved ones who are now in the spirit world, and ourselves. Spirit communication is a wonderful method of connection between the two worlds, uniting those who reside in the realms of spirit with those who exist in the physical body.

This link allows spirit beings to teach, guide and give messages of love and support to those with whom they connect in the material world. Communion is linked with the idea of community and it is with others in our spiritual family that we can share feelings and emotions in communion, whilst communication allows the transmission of ideas, concepts and information.

The Latin word *communio* means mutual participation, thus the Communion of Spirits can be viewed in several ways. There is the belief that we can share a fellowship of thought, feeling and aspiration that extends far beyond anything we can express in words. We speak of 'communing with nature,' moving away totally from the verbal expression of ideas to a point where our spiritual heart reacts and responds to feeling and emotion. A sunset, the song of a bird, the beauty of a flower, the ecstasy of music – such experiences produce responses that are felt, yet cannot adequately be conveyed in words. We cannot scientifically analyse such feelings and reactions, we cannot quantify or measure them, yet we would not question their existence or their importance.

There is but one existence. That which exists cannot be destroyed and the spirit within can never be extinguished, whether it is in an individualised form or in the wider sense as part of the Spirit-Energy vibration. Matter may change its form but the energy it contains – the vital element of existence – will find another vehicle through which it can express itself and through which it can establish and maintain contact with its environment, whatever manner of environment that may be.

It is usually the accumulation of evidential messages that support known facts that gives us our personal conviction that we survive in spirit form. Such information passed to us from the spirit world confirms that our loved ones continue to exist and that they are living a conscious, active spiritual life. That being the reality, we can then extend our understanding to accept the fact that those same loved ones are capable of being supportive influences on our lives after they have departed from the physical plane of existence.

From the information contained in spirit messages we also know that our loved ones who have passed to spirit continue to watch over us and have unending concern for our welfare. It is a delight to the heart to be reassured of their continuing care, so much so that with their support we are strengthened and sustained on our journey throughout the adversities of earthly life. With the help of spirit we are given the courage to overcome conditions that are not conducive to good health, happiness and potential. We should be forever thankful for the care and compassion expressed by our spirit friends through this channel of spiritual energy.

One widely held view of communion is that it is intended to raise up the thoughts and aspirations of people to help them embrace the teachings of the masters and leaders in whom they believe. Many words of wisdom and grace have been given to mankind from the spirit world, with spirit communication being the channel for teachings concerning the purpose of life, soul progression and spiritual evolution. Communion in the Spiritualist sense is intended to encourage people to open their hearts and minds to the eternal truth that they are in essence spiritual beings. In acknowledging this they will come to understand their own spiritual nature and accept that, in refining their spiritual sensitivity, the world for them will begin to take on a new order. As people acknowledge their fundamental spiritual condition they will comprehend that spirituality does not apply to them alone but to everyone, regardless of whether or not it is consciously acknowledged by the individual. As the dawning of spiritual truth begins to illuminate the human mind, people will come to understand that essential links unite human beings with the forces of all life.

In our physical lives we accept that many experiences will be gathered and they will not pass away into dust but remain with us when we pass to the spirit world. God intended us to lead good, productive lives with the object of advancing our spirituality and

31

humanity in harmony with our fellow travellers in life. What can be more natural, therefore, than that when we pass to spirit we will want to use the knowledge and experience we have acquired to enhance not only our own spiritual progression but also that of others?

If we accept that communion with nature is a natural and normal process it is then no great leap of the imagination to accept that we can also commune with Spirit. The Father God/Mother Earth/Mother Nature concept of the Creator is common to many forms of religious philosophy, so it must follow that if we can make a spiritual link with one part of this life-force, then why not with the whole of it? In our sharing in common the feelings, emotions and fellowship of other men we cannot exclude the bond between the individualised aspect of spirit and the Great Spirit Itself. In response to the finer aspirations that lie deep within each of us we can, through the Higher Being at our very core, receive guidance, aid and succour for our spirits. Although we accept objectively that our present level of knowledge and wisdom limits what we can consciously understand, subjectively we know that our potential is without boundary and that we are creatures of infinite possibility.

We must accept, however, that at our present level of development we still have a long way to go. To expect to receive inspiration directly from the Ultimate Source of all knowledge and wisdom is to set our sights somewhat high. In simple terms, the inspirational energy directed to us needs to be changed to a level that will enable us to receive it. It follows, therefore, that the finessing of the spiritual vibrations must allow us not only to receive information but also to understand and react to it. Just as a transformer is needed to change the voltage of electrical energy, so is there a requirement to alter spiritual vibrations of pure love and wisdom to a vibrational range that can be assimilated by human hearts and minds. This vibrational range will be dependent upon the level of spiritual development of the individual for whom the communication is intended.

We are fortunate indeed that spirit communicators are adept in adjusting their vibrations to meet ours at an appropriate level to facilitate good, inspirational connections. The potential to commune is within us all, but the degree of success will vary considerably according to the innate natural ability of the individual. It does not necessarily follow that by accepting Spiritualist belief and becoming a Spiritualist one can automatically commune with spirit.

It must be understood that the communication we have with those in the spirit world does not replace or interfere with the responsibility we have for the decisions we make in our lives. The experiences we have will always be the result of our own thoughts, decisions and actions, but in the same way that all good parents help and encourage their children to achieve the best they can, so we acknowledge that our Father-Mother God can help us. In allowing spirit communication to take place between us and those who have gone before the Great Spirit has provided for us the same help and encouragement that we have given to our own children.

The Ministry of Angels

Ministering angels can be understood in their role as the divine helpers of God through whose agency He makes known His purpose and will. Angels serve God's cause and act on His authority for the good of His other creations. Angels have not existed on Earth in physical form but are immortal, supernal beings of the purest spiritual existence.

The primary function of angels is to honour and serve God, but they also have a secondary role in which they act as His emissaries to mankind. They fulfil this role by giving protection, support and encouragement to human beings on their journey through life. These messengers of God are bringers of love and wisdom and they convey to us a greater understanding of our own spiritual nature and the spiritual universe. They give us an awareness of God's Plan and of our personal role within that Plan. They show us the pathway that will best advance our spiritual progression.

We are perhaps most familiar with what is known as the guardian angel. This term applies to those angels who take on the special responsibility of helping us as individuals to achieve the true purpose for our stay on earth. Guardian angels come close to us when we are in trouble or need. They seek to assist us by offering their protection and support, bringing with them perfect love for easement of our distress. They bring the light of eternal truth for our upliftment and they rejoice when we are happy and fulfilled.

In the world of spirit there are many levels of experience and accumulated wisdom that can be accessed by angelic messengers. Many people on Earth have attested to the changes that have occurred in their lives as a direct result of angelic intervention. Angelic influences have been known to bring about beneficial effects on individual situations at times of great danger, need or illness. They also try to bring their influences to the wider world for the betterment of the human condition.

It must be understood, however, that although angelic intervention is for our benefit, it does not interfere with the responsibility we have to conduct our lives in accordance with our conscience. That responsibility is ours alone to bear, but the angelic energy force is there to help and support us in our endeavours.

We are thus doubly blessed in having the loving care of our spirit helpers and the protection and support of supernal beings from the highest spheres of existence. It is a great comfort to know that as we walk the pathway of earthly life there is help available to us from both the spiritual and celestial realms. With the support and encouragement of these two loving aspects of God's creation we are able to get through the struggles of ordinary human life. We know that with the guidance of compassionate spiritual and angelic beings we shall move towards fulfilment of the purpose for which our earthly lives were intended.

The Third Principle of Spiritualism upholds the human experience of linking with individual spirits and higher beings and affirms that we can both commune and communicate with them. We know, rather than believe, that life continues after physical death and that living people can communicate with those who no longer inhabit the physical body. Through personal experience and close, detailed examination of the evidence Spiritualists have individually and collectively reached a point where they can say that survival of the spirit and communication from the spirit world have been proved to their satisfaction.

The philosophy of Spiritualism is based on the simple concept that there is a great creative force which we term God. Humankind is part of that energy force and can never be separated from it. In addition, in the right circumstances people can communicate with other individualised parts of that energy force. Having examined all the possibilities, Spiritualists have come to the conclusion that this is the most logical and natural way in which to interpret the evidence they have studied. There is nothing hidden, nor is there anything that comes from a source other than God.

From time immemorial man has linked with the spirit world to communicate with his ancestors and spirit masters of wisdom and truth. Spiritualists continue that tradition and offer evidence of survival of physical death. It is up to the individual to decide for himself whether that evidence constitutes proof of the continuity of life. The Great Spirit has given each of us the talent and ability needed to enable us to make our own decisions of conscience. It would therefore be ungracious to allow other people to make such decisions for us rather than use that God-given ability to decide for ourselves.

No earthly intermediary is needed, be it person, book, place or doctrine, to give reassurance that there is continuity of life after physical death. All that is needed is an open mind and a loving heart to enable progression to higher spiritual values. Our human experience tells us that we do indeed commune with the spiritual energies and forces around us and that we are inspired by music, art, beauty and love. We happily communicate with our families, friends and loved ones whilst on Earth and the change of perspective and experience called death does not alter that. Love, compassion and care continue from this world to the next. Through spiritual communion we know that on our earthly journey we do not walk alone.

Fourth Principle

The Continuous Existence of the Human Soul

The Continuous Existence of the Human Soul

The Fourth Principle of Spiritualism affirms the belief that life continues beyond physical existence. In considering the idea of continuous existence the starting-point on this journey of exploration and understanding is an appreciation that there is a divine life-force which created mankind and which sustains and maintains it. Man is an integral part of this divine life-force and it is as impossible to consider this force never having been in existence as it is to consider its ever ceasing to exist. It is, because of its nature, continuous. If God is continuous and mankind is an inseparable part of God, then man can do nothing other than accept the idea that human life also is continuous.

Many religious philosophies other than Spiritualism accept the concept of life after death but few accept, as Spiritualism does, that the human spirit continues to progress after the transition called death. In support of this claim Spiritualists have through observation and experiment gathered together empirical evidence that supports the concept of life after death. It is this accumulation of evidence that forms the basis of the claim of Spiritualism for survival of human consciousness and identity after death.

Evidence of survival has been demonstrated over many years to make the case for continuous existence. Spirit communicators and spirit phenomena of many kinds have provided strong, corroborative evidence for both scientific investigators and laymen alike. Spirit activity has been monitored under careful scrutiny by groups of dedicated people who have undertaken many years of patient research to produce results that can be verified and corroborated. This evidence has confirmed that the soul retains its consciousness, intellect, character and personality after the death of the physical body. It has also been possible through spirit communication to receive information that validates personal attributes and distinguishing characteristics, thus authenticating the identities of discarnate spirits. The aspects of personality which define each of us as an individual – emotions, memories, hopes, ambitions, loves, fears, sense of humour and so forth – remain an integral part of us. These distinctive characteristics are still recognisable to us and to those with whom we have had contact during the various stages of life. Convincing, descriptive detail can therefore be conveyed from the discarnate to the incarnate by way of spirit communication, confirming the identity of the communicating spirit entity. It is nevertheless incumbent upon each of us to come to our own conclusions as to the validity of the evidence provided from the etheric realms, and spirit would not wish it otherwise.

If we are to accept that life continues to exist, then we must establish what it is that continues to exist. The soul and spirit are considered to be one and the same, that is, the immortal spiritual component of a living being. It is this element that survives separation from the earthly body. The immortal spiritual component that is the soul/spirit encompasses the development and evolution that has been attained thus far and expresses the person in its entirety. Each of us is born as a spirit of love, innocence and purity and as a conscious being. Through our experiences of human life we develop the character and personality traits that define us. It is this consciousness that we take with us after transition, and these distinguishing aspects and features of the self that we convey through spirit communication.

The Fourth Principle specifies the 'human soul' and, as Spiritualists, we certainly accept that each human being who has ever lived on earth or will live here in the future will continue in existence to the end of time. It could also be predicated that continuous existence is not the exclusive province of mankind and that other forms of life also continue to exist beyond death. It could therefore be said that whatever lives will share in this continuity of existence. This does not necessarily mean that each individualised form of life will continue in the same form forever. It may well be that some will, at the termination of their present earthly existence, continue in a different form. What we accept is that the spirit of each and every form of life will be maintained, though its nature and form may well change.

The concept of continuity contains within it the idea of growth, increased understanding and wisdom. If we came to know all the answers during the human passage of life, where would we find the challenges and opportunities of the future that encourage intellectual development and spiritual evolution?

Because of the very nature of what comes after physical existence it is almost impossible to put into perspective what future spheres of life will be like or how we will take part in them. How do we understand ideas of time, space, and movement when we have different reference points from which to relate our understanding? If we had always lived deep in the ocean, under enormous pressure, in a completely wet environment, we would find it very hard to understand what it would be like to live on land in dry conditions and at a fraction of the pressure. The conditions in the next part of life are even more different from those under which we live here and now, so it is beyond our comprehension to fully grasp the immensity and infinity of such an environment.

For this reason, Spiritualists do not give definitive answers to questions such as 'What is it like in the spirit world?' or 'What will happen to me when I die and where shall I be?' The knowledge we have is based on information passed to us by those who have experienced the change called death. We accept that each person prepares on earth, by the manner in which he lives life here, the place in which he will find himself after death. For some, it will be a happy place where they will be surrounded by friends and by love, whilst for others it will be a place as dark as that which they left behind in their physical existence.

Nevertheless, what we do understand is that, however dark the place a person has prepared or created for himself, there is always the opportunity for him to move to a place of light because, even though he may not want to accept his surroundings, there is always, without exception, love around him. In such circumstances a person is encompassed by beings of light and love whose purpose is to help every individual move forward to a better and happier place. No one is ever cut off from the all-embracing love of the God Force.

It matters not how someone has been judged by mankind or how he has judged himself, for everyone has within him that infinite spark of divinity, that element of God which expresses his true spiritual self. Spiritual evolution is inexorable. We cannot halt it; we may resist it for a long period of time but eventually the motivation to move forward will arise, whether prompted from within or by external spiritual pressure. There is an inevitability about progression. In time, and it may be a long time in earthly terms, every person will 'see the light' and know that he wants to move towards it and into it. There is never compulsion, just loving encouragement. Nothing in the universe remains permanently static and God ensures that everything moves on.

That we continue in some form beyond human earthly existence is not a new concept. It is known that many ancient peoples and ancient religious beliefs were confident of continued spiritual existence after death. The ancients accepted as natural that their ancestors survived the change from the incarnate state to the discarnate. They also accepted that their physically deceased, but spiritually surviving, ancestors had the ability to influence events affecting those still living on earth. Ancient peoples respected their ancestors in spirit in the same way as they had done when those forebears were in their earthly existence. This concept can still be seen in religious philosophies across the world today. It can be said, however, that Spiritualism is distinguishable from other philosophies by its acceptance and practice of spirit communication, with information and guidance being transmitted from the spirit world to earthly recipients.

Some people believe that in accepting help from those who have gone before we take away our right to live our lives in our own way. The response to this is that God in His wisdom has granted us free will in all aspects of life, so we can choose to heed or ignore the help offered. When we are in possession of the facts of a particular situation it is up to us to undertake an analysis and make a decision based on our own judgment. Information from those in the realms of spirit is intended to help us by providing guidance that will direct us toward the best conclusion. Such help will not usurp our right to make a decision and we will still bear the consequences of our actions. We cannot place on the shoulders of others responsibility for the outcome of decisions we make.

How individual growth will be achieved is an area in which human beings have very limited experience. We understand that there will be endless opportunities for us in which to expand love and knowledge, but whether these opportunities lie solely in moving forward by a direct route or by re-visiting areas previously experienced is not known. We should always be open to learn more from all sources and be prepared to change our opinions, even those that have been deeply held for a long time, should our increased experience and expanded knowledge lead us to new conclusions.

Any such conclusion is really what we know and understand at a particular time. Spiritualist philosophy is based on the realisation that there are no real conclusions because nothing has been, or ever will be, concluded. Everything moves on. The views we hold are dependent on the stage we are at in our lives at any given moment. We do not have all the answers, for we have not even scratched the surface of knowing all the questions. We move forward in our quest to find the meaning of life and our place within that life. There is no heaven and no hell – only situations in which we find ourselves as a result of our own thoughts, words and actions. We will reap what we sow and this is important in thinking of the continuous aspect of life.

Belief systems, conscious actions, desires, hopes, aspirations, acceptance or rejection – none of these will influence or affect the fact of the continuity of life. Spiritualism has at the core of its philosophy the acceptance of the idea that everyone shares this continuity. A person will not die in the sense that he will cease to exist; nothing will change that. There are established and inescapable laws of both the physical world and the spiritual world. For example, a man may want, or try, to believe that if he puts water in a kettle and places it on a flame and leaves it, the water will not boil. Whatever one's personal wishes, nature is such that the water will boil. Continuous existence is like that – it is an inevitable consequence and part of the nature of life. A person cannot 'not die' nor can he 'not continue'. There is a saying that 'you cannot die for the life of you' and that sums up the Spiritualist position.

What an individual can influence, however, is the quality of the life he will move on to after death. He should live physical life based on the higher qualities suggested by all religious philosophies – a life in which he has love and respect for himself and others, demands the best for himself and others and seeks to achieve the best for himself whilst helping others to achieve what is best for them. As individuals we are able to make decisions for and control only one

43

life – our own. We can nevertheless greatly influence the lives of others by example, good or bad, and by service or disservice to other individuals and communities.

For life to have true meaning it must have purpose. That purpose is served by acknowledging the continuity of life and that God in His wisdom allows us to take with us beyond physical death all that we have experienced in life. In this way we continue to be what we created during our physical lives. It would seem illogical that our Creator would see a human life as three score years and ten, then simply return it to dust. What would be the point? All the talents, the experiences and wisdom a person had gained from life surely cannot have been for nothing.

The Fourth Principle of Spiritualism, The Continuous Existence of the Human Soul, offers both an opportunity and a challenge for the future and, just as importantly, for the present. What we do now is preparing for us the life we will enjoy or endure in our continued existence. No one else can do it for us. The future, be it in our present physical form or after death in a non-physical form, starts from this moment. We must live for today while we prepare for tomorrow. We should create the heaven we want by opening our hearts to the love around us and by passing it on to those who, as yet, lack our knowledge, wisdom and compassion. In that way life after death will be exciting, challenging and rewarding.

The continuous existence of the human soul is the fulfilment of God's implied promise in His creation of human life. We should welcome it, embrace it and enjoy it. We should live life to the fullest and the best now, and when the future is upon us, simply continue to live.

Fifth Principle

Personal Responsibility

Personal Responsibility

Earlier Principles have shown that Spiritualism accepts the existence of a Supreme Power as the central platform of its philosophy. These Principles have then indicated how the relationship between the Supreme Power and its creations is understood in Spiritualism. The Principles have shown what could be described as the laws of existence – the rights of every living being.

The Fifth Principle of Spiritualism is important because the personal responsibility we accept for our actions during our physical lives is a key indicator of who and what we are. The quality of the person, character and spirit is determined by what is done and what is thought by an individual while he walks the earthly pathway of life. The sum total of what we are as soul and spirit is what we take to the spirit world. This is our spiritual identity. It will be recognised as being everything we have worked towards making of ourselves at that point in our spiritual evolution. When we pass over to the other side of life, those who also inhabit the spirit realms will be able to see the quality of who and what we are and will be able to relate to us accordingly.

Although the Fifth Principle refers to Personal Responsibility, it is not intended to convey that, provided we are satisfied with our behaviour, we are free to ignore the effect our actions have on others. We are required not only to look at how our thoughts and actions affect our direct relationships but also the effect our behaviour will have on the rest of humankind in general. Although each of us is an individual, the outcome of our thoughts and actions will reflect on others in one way or another. We must be aware that, whilst what we do may further our personal cause, it might also be detrimental to others.

Divine Law, which operates throughout the universe, is unchangeable and inescapable. One aspect of Divine Law is the Law of Cause and Effect, which is easily understood and succinctly expressed in the phrase 'As you sow, so shall you reap'. If we are conscious of the many aspects of Divine Law, in accepting personal responsibility we are more likely to make decisions for the right reasons.

Having accepted the idea that man is at the apex of creation on earth, we also accept the special role he has to play. Man is the thinking being who has the ability to reason, make logical decisions and then take the required action. He has been given rights, the counterbalance of which is responsibility. Each person carries Personal Responsibility.

It is sometimes said that the Fifth Principle indicates that we have free will. But is this really the case? What we usually have is choice, with a variety of opportunities presented that allow us to decide what to do in any given circumstance. For instance, if we were driving in the countryside and approached a T-junction, we could go only one of two ways – left or right. To go straight on would not be an option because there is no road ahead. We could decide to drive across the field in front of us but that would be impractical and unlikely, so the third option would not really be feasible. It would appear, therefore, that in certain situations several possible directions could be taken but common sense and experience tell us that the options are limited.

When we have a choice between options the responsibility is ours as to which we choose. There are no absolutes and each situation must be looked at in its own light. For instance, whilst stealing would generally be adjudged to be a fault rather than a virtue, is the penniless mother who steals food for her children guilty of a crime? Perhaps there is a greater good which extends above and beyond normal convention. Whatever the fault or crime, and however serious it may be, all the circumstances of the individual concerned should be considered. This is not to excuse or justify an action of any nature, however bad, but to ensure that we do not make a judgment without being aware of everything surrounding that action.

Free will, therefore, is not an absolute but a relative concept that might well depend on forces over which we have no control. It may be that at a point in the future people will come to understand and use those forces. The development of mankind over the centuries suggests that such a moment will arrive, but it has yet to be reached. Personal responsibility can, at times, be a heavy burden to carry but is nevertheless rewarding in the longer term. Sometimes the difficulties of life can test our physical, mental and emotional strengths to the limit but it is how we react to such trials that mould and form the spiritual self. The complexities of modern society can place a great strain on an individual and make demands that have to be met and answered physically, mentally and spiritually. When we are placed in positions of moral and spiritual crisis during our lifetime, the decisions we make and the actions we take are directly related to our spiritual growth. Intention is therefore the key to whatever action we take.

If personal responsibility allows us to recognise our strengths and weaknesses, our successes and failures, then our lives with all their frailties and problems are truly under our control. Mistakes are ours to make as long as we realise that in making them others may be affected. We do not always know how or when the effects of our mistakes may materialise in the lives of others.

Much of life is shaped by the way we were brought up and by the standards that were instilled into us as children. What we may not realise is that, based upon our upbringing and experience of life, we can affect our children and they in turn their children. We do not know how far into the future the things we were taught, and which we in turn taught others, may be of influence. We touch many more lives than we realise, both in the present and the future.

Throughout our lives we make decisions, many of which are advantageous to ourselves, whilst many, when viewed in hindsight, will be seen as having been somewhat less than beneficial. In addition to the quality and effect of these decisions on our own lives, consideration must be given to the effects that our actions will have upon the lives of others. What we do may have far-reaching consequences of which we are unaware, touching people who would not normally be expected to come into our personal domain.

For example, the actions of an individual who decides to drive after drinking and then has an accident which kills or maims someone else will have both short- and long-term consequences. This applies not only to those directly involved but also to their families, friends, colleagues and the many other people with whom they are connected. The length of time for which these people will be affected will vary – in the case of family it will last for years or even decades, whilst for others the effect will be transitory. However, memories of the trauma may continue to influence lives and decisions long after the event itself has faded from the forefront of public consciousness.

Not everything we do is as dramatic as the drink-drive situation but that example serves to indicate how what we do affects us and others, shaping future lives, actions and pathways. Because of the gravity of possible consequences it is important that we think and consider for as long as necessary before we act. We can take great strides forward in understanding our motives and ourselves by examining and questioning what we have done. It is comforting to know that spirit helpers will always be there to support us when we falter and also to encourage us towards a finer and better pathway. With their help and our own firmness of purpose we will be able to achieve our true spiritual potential.

Let us now consider the difference in magnitude between personal decisions, which are comparatively limited in effect, and national or global decisions that affect whole populations. Even for the ordinary amongst us the seemingly simplest of choices can have far-reaching consequences. To travel by car, bus or train does not seem to be a life-changing decision but should there be an accident the decision suddenly takes on a vastly different perspective. The seemingly minor act of choosing between three modes of transport could in fact turn out to be a crucial decision with profoundly life-changing consequences both to ourselves and to others.

Decisions such as these can nevertheless be seen to be very different in magnitude from decisions made by leaders of nations who control the lives of millions of people. The ethical approach should nevertheless be the same. The more power and responsibility a person holds, the longer and harder should be the task of preparing the mind to make momentous decisions. Individuals who wield great power, control or authority bear a very heavy burden, which should make them mindful of their actions and responsibilities in a global context. The lives and well-being of their own people and possibly of other nations of the world depend on the competent exercise of personal responsibility. There is thus a profound need for leaders to ensure that they make ethically and morally correct decisions when deliberating on national and international affairs.

Having considered the importance of decision-making as part of personal responsibility, there is another aspect also to be considered – that of language and rhetoric. The spoken word can have far-reaching effects on the lives of individuals, communities and nations. The power of words to please or hurt is immense and a word once uttered cannot be taken back. Everyone should be aware of the power of words and how positive or negative they can be. The supportive words we say to family, friends and acquaintances may inspire them to achieve things they thought impossible of themselves. On the other hand, confidence may be destroyed, feelings shattered and immense emotional pain caused by ill-chosen words or angry outbursts.

If we consider once again the power of national leaders, there will be many instances which can be brought to mind of heroic statesmen giving courage to their people in times of national distress. It will also be easy to recall cases of disturbing rhetoric given by leaders of dubious intent who wish to incite their people to follow a morally questionable pathway. The power of the spoken word is great and must be used with the greatest of care and consideration.

Let us now turn to the written word, which also has the power to influence others in a positive or negative manner. The effects of newspaper articles, for example, can influence countless lives and decisions because there is a tendency to accept that what is written has some particular validity. We may say that we never believe what appears in the press but few can totally disregard the content of newspaper columns. We may think we act on the principle of 'innocent until proven guilty' and always give someone the benefit of the doubt, but perhaps we tend at times also to think 'no smoke without fire'.

If we could generate thoughts of only a positive nature full of care, respect and love, then the world would be so much better than it is now. Sadly, our lack of understanding and wisdom means that such an ideal is little more than a hope for the future. The reality of life is that we all think thoughts tinged with, or influenced by, our preconceived ideas or deficient knowledge, understanding, and lack of respect for others. Our childhood upbringing, education, religion, society and other influences also play a part in how our decisions are reached. The vast majority of people want to do what is right and best, but however hard they try they do not always succeed, because putting into practice higher ideals is not always easy. The reason for this is not difficult to understand, because mankind is in the process of a very long period of development. To think that we are at a level where our decisions will always reflect the highest and noblest ambitions is to take a step back from reality, but we must continue to reach out for the ultimate in truth and divine enlightenment.

The state of the world is not inevitable and beyond our control and, rather than mere acceptance of the status quo, we have the power to drive forward the changes we see as beneficial. We simply need the will to do so.

We should be aware that it is not only what we do that is important but also the intention behind the action. Our responsibility is to try as hard as possible to be the very best we can, yet we must never demand of ourselves more than we are capable of achieving. We should always remember that we are human, with all the limitations to be expected of the physical state. Our constrained knowledge and understanding of the Force we call God and of His intentions for us mean that we will never be condemned for failure.

Personal Responsibility gives us the strength to take command of our lives whilst realising that we are important in God's plan. There is no such thing as someone born into life without purpose, but to recognise that purpose and do what is inherently right takes time and courage to implement. From the highest to the lowest, all are equal in the eyes of God, all are capable of great deeds of love and compassion or of creating trouble and strife. There is no fundamental difference between ordinary people and the great teachers of life – those teachers who change the thinking of communities and society and whose message has often reached the wider world in order to change mankind. These great masters, having recognised the task they had been given to perform, proceeded to take responsibility for their role in the fulfilment of God's plan.

The concept of Personal Responsibility sets Spiritualist philosophy apart from many other religious beliefs. By accepting the idea that we sow what we reap we move away from the precept that we can be redeemed from sin. We are not left at the mercy of a vengeful God, needing to be saved by some agency that will intercede on our behalf. By accepting responsibility for what we do, say and think we accept the great respect that God has shown us. This God of Love, Justice and Honour bestows these same qualities upon us. We come to understand that respect for ourselves, our fellow beings and the Great Spirit is fundamental to our progression.

We recognise that all human life, whatever its gender or background, has been created by the God Energy. Those who seek to deny the rights and opportunities of any section within humankind do themselves, their fellow human beings and God an injustice. We must always defend the right of people to be given respect and to be allowed to think and act for themselves.

We can make decisions for only one life, our own, but personal progress can be enhanced by the manner in which we relate to others and interact with all those we meet, however fleetingly, on our journey through life.

The Fifth Principle can be summarised as follows: -

Individual Responsibility - The way we interact directly with loved ones, relatives and friends.

Group Responsibility - The way we act and engage in the local community.

Collective Responsibility - The view we have of the world and what we can contribute to alleviate the pain and suffering of others, and also to be generally constructive and beneficial to mankind, the environment and the animal kingdom.

God has entrusted us with Personal Responsibility. Let us endeavour to live up to this trust and His, and our, highest ideals and purpose.

Sixth Principle

Compensation and Retribution Hereafter for all the Good and Evil Deeds done on Earth

Compensation and Retribution Hereafter for all the Good and Evil Deeds done on Earth

At first glance it may seem that the meaning behind the Sixth Principle is not difficult to appreciate: that we will be rewarded or punished for what we have done or, in other words, we reap what we sow. There is, however, a need to go beyond this somewhat simplistic idea when developing an understanding of the total package represented by the Seven Principles. In considering the Sixth Principle, any thought of punishment must not be equated with that which we see applied in the courts on a daily basis.

The ultimate judgment on our behavioural history is not made by others but by ourselves. It is spiritual retribution that we bring on our heads if our conduct falls below expected standards, and spiritual compensation if we reach or exceed those standards. Under the law of the land some people may escape punishment or penalty, but under Natural Law they are answerable for what they have done and will never be able to escape the consequences of their actions. The Sixth Principle indicates that the scales of spiritual justice are inevitably weighed, with the concepts of fairness and equity being brought into balance.

How many times have we heard it said, 'He got away with it. Life is so unfair.'? In some cases it may appear that a person has indeed escaped punishment for a crime he has committed. However, all is not necessarily as it may seem. In compensation and retribution it is assured that no one will get away with anything; all actions and behaviour, whether good or bad, ultimately will be accounted for. God's concern is for our spiritual progression. He does not express approval or disapproval of our actions because the operation of Natural Law will ultimately deliver Divine Justice.

There will always be those who rail against any law, whether man-made or spiritual, when it interferes with their intention to attain an enhanced position in life or to gain advantage over others. In such cases it is often difficult to see justice at work, but it is an incontrovertible truth of spiritual law that, no matter who they are, no one can escape Divine Justice.

Everyone will one day see the error of their ways and have to confront themselves and the full implications of their actions. What may appear to have been an injustice in the application of judicial law in earthly life will not in spirit life escape the operation of Divine Law.

If on passing to the spirit world we do not like the situation in which we find ourselves, we shall eventually come to the realisation that we alone have created the condition of our spiritual surroundings. We shall then be given the chance to create a better state of existence by acknowledging past errors and determining the best way forward. A more advanced level of spiritual progression can only be achieved through understanding what we have done and in seeking to atone for the errors and poor behaviour that we have perpetrated. Nobody else can do this for us – the hard work of spiritual refinement is entirely up to the individual concerned. It must be understood, however, that in every case unfailing support and guidance will be given by spirit teachers and masters whose purpose is to help us to achieve our true spiritual potential.

It has been established in previous Principles that Spiritualists view God as the Supreme Being, Who is all-powerful and all-knowing. Power brings the opportunity to control, be this in a benign or an authoritarian manner. Used in an authoritarian way it could involve a 'carrot and stick' approach – 'Do things as I wish and you will be rewarded; do things that displease me and you will be punished.' There is, however, an additional concept in the Spiritualist view of God: not only is He all-powerful and all-knowing but He is also all-love. If we accept this additional element, then we understand that punishment (causing someone to suffer, or imposing a penalty for an offence) is totally alien to the nature of God.

In the chapter on the Fifth Principle it has clearly been shown that we have personal responsibility for our own lives. We are accountable for all our actions, thoughts and motives because they are ours and ours alone. This applies to the physical life as well as to the spiritual life. In the physical world, when the law is broken the authorities responsible for legal restitution will prosecute and, depending on the view of the courts, administer punishment accordingly. Spiritual law is different insofar as there are no courts and no judges.

We are the only ones who know the reasons for our actions and the motives behind those actions. When we are in a position to comprehend the full implications of what we have done, we will be encouraged by more enlightened spirit beings to evaluate our behaviour and make spiritual restitution in accordance with spiritual law.

In the spirit world there is no heaven or hell, only levels of spiritual evolution and degrees of spiritual development. When we pass from this world to the next we gravitate to the level of spiritual understanding we have achieved at that point. We cannot move to a higher level than the one we have earned thus far and it is at this juncture that guidance from spirit masters will help us to unfold and reveal our higher selves. We have the choice to remain where we are or to acquire more learning and move onward. The choice we make determines how our prospective spiritual enlightenment is to proceed, either by forward movement or stasis.

Onward progress is essential if the light of our spiritual refinement is to be enhanced and higher spiritual vibrations achieved. Progress will not be made without effort and express intention on our part, and we must be prepared to work hard to earn the spiritual advancement to which we aspire. Any endeavour we undertake for the advancement of personal spiritual progress will require dedication of purpose. Deep examination of personal motivation will be necessary in respect of former deeds. We will not be able to dismiss or turn aside from what we have done but will have to face squarely all the actions of our physical lives and the consequences that have arisen from them. Everything will be considered and taken into account in order to achieve spiritual balance.

In the examination and review of the earthly lives we have led many of us will initially link compensation with good deeds, whilst associating retribution with evil deeds. Both these words are, however, closely linked with the same concept and we must understand that there is more behind the Sixth Principle than at first appears evident. It should be remembered that 'compensation' comes from the verb 'to compensate'. To compensate for something indicates seeking to recompense or make amends for what has happened. We try to make amends for those issues we think of as having had an adverse effect on others, seeking to put things right.

It may also be helpful if we consider another aspect of compensation. This lies in the word 'counterbalance'. If we bring counterbalance into our understanding we see a different aspect added to the meaning of compensation. We move from reward and punishment to seeing that for any and every action there must be a counterbalancing reaction. Science tells us that, in physical terms, for every action there is a corresponding and equal reaction. We can transfer this same idea to our understanding of the Sixth Principle: every action we take has a counterbalancing reaction, equal in strength, intensity and outcome.

We will not be rewarded or punished for the reactions in others; we will see the counterbalancing effects in our own lives and on our own spiritual progression and development. The concept of there being two opposing forces, good and evil, is removed, leaving us with the knowledge that for whatever we do, whatever action we cause to happen, there will be a reaction within our own lives and inner spiritual nature.

There may also be reaction in and on other beings, although it must be understood that what we do relates primarily to one life – our own. That is the only life over which we have any real control. The responses that our actions create within others become the responsibility of those individuals. Their responses in turn will influence their own personal growth and progression. It can be seen, therefore, that how we and they react is the personal responsibility of every individual involved and the nature of the response will influence the manner and rate of spiritual development of each person.

The Sixth Principle also refers to the hereafter, so we must look at definitions of this word. One dictionary definition is: in the world to come (after death). There is probably an immediate feeling that when we use 'hereafter' in this context we are referring to what will follow this stage of life, the period that comes after death.

However, if we look at another definition – in fact the primary dictionary definition – we see that it talks of: from now on; in the future. Taken in that light, we can view the implications of the Sixth Principle in a very different way. The reaction or counterbalancing process begins not only after death but at any time from now on. That future starts the instant after performance of the action, thus the counterbalancing procedure may start as soon as the action has taken place.

How many times have we done something and then wanted to change it immediately, never mind at some distant moment? This clearly shows that we are, or can be, aware of the need to make amends or counterbalance an action at any time after the action has been performed. There is no implication in the Sixth Principle that the act of compensation will have to wait until we are in the next phase of life. We cannot use the wording of the Principle as a justification for thinking that things will be sorted out after the process of death and that while we are in the physical period of life we can simply carry on without regard for the immediacy of the consequences of our actions.

When our thoughts, actions and motives are based on the highest of ideals, that fact will be acknowledged through deductive reasoning as compensation. When our thoughts, actions and motives are based on self-interest and greed, with resultant detriment to others, a penalty will be paid in the form of retribution. This does not mean that we will go to hell. We shall instead be given the opportunity to understand what we have done and, if it is our wish, to atone for those transgressions. All actions in life are part of the experience that is intended to influence our spiritual development. We should remember, however, that we are only human and will therefore make mistakes as we cope with the stresses and adversities of life. 'To err is human', as the saying goes, and error is thus inevitable. We make mistakes for a variety of reasons, sometimes through simple human weakness and sometimes because we fail to understand the full spiritual implications of our errors.

In considering the Sixth Principle we have mainly looked at deeds or actions, but consideration should also be given to another aspect – the power of words. Who has not been hurt by words as much as actions? Who has not been uplifted, strengthened,

61

encouraged or helped by words as much as actions? The power of words is enormous. They have the power to influence and affect the feelings and behaviour of ourselves and others, not only immediately after they have been uttered but in some cases for many years to come.

It is therefore essential to comprehend that the thoughts and intentions behind both words and actions are of great importance. We may do something wrong through ignorance or lack of awareness when in fact we are truly trying to do good. In the counterbalancing process the intent will have a tremendous bearing on both the reaction and how it is carried out. If our thoughts and intentions are of a high nature, then even though we may get things wrong, we will still realise when we review our past actions that they had a positive quality, even if the results may have been less than satisfactory. Every thought, word and deed produces a result that can be a learning process.

In the context of the Sixth Principle, when we examine the meaning of the word 'good' it would seem reasonable to talk of that which is beneficial or morally right, both to ourselves and to others. Also in the context of this Principle we can define evil as being that which is unfavourable or which brings disadvantage or misfortune to ourselves and to others. Spiritualists view good and evil as being different sides of the same coin, or different points along the same scale of measurement. Put in another way, good and evil are counterbalancing aspects of the same force.

Spiritualists do not accept that there are two opposing forces, one good (emanating from God) and the other evil (coming from the Devil). Having established the Spiritualist concept of God as being the all-powerful, all-knowing and all-loving Ultimate Being, it becomes impossible to accept that there can be another force existing in opposition to God. To accept such a concept is to negate all ideas of a Supreme Being Which has created and established the universe and all that exists within it.

When the Sixth Principle refers to 'good and evil deeds' it relates to two aspects: (i) those things which are beneficial and produce positive and progressive responses and encourage personal growth and development; (ii) those things which cause harm and misfortune and produce negative responses or limit the rate of progression of ourselves and others. Even given these general concepts we nevertheless have to remember that good and evil are not straightforwardly black or white, but shades of grey. There are no absolutes – every action must be judged on its individual merits. What may appear to be wrong in the general sense may take on a different aspect when the complete background relating to a particular situation is known.

There is no need to concern ourselves with a vengeful God who will weigh up the good with the bad in our lives and adjudicate upon our destination. Heaven and hell can be understood as varying states of mind and spiritual development, not actual locations. The operation of Natural Law ensures accountability through compensation and retribution and is the ultimate reckoning of the omissions and commissions of our lives. We prepare the state into which we move after death by the way in which we live now and by the manner in which we respond to the lessons undertaken. The justice we impose upon ourselves governs our personal spiritual development and the way in which it is revealed is in the intensity of our spiritual illumination.

Here and now we are creating our future existence in the spirit world. As we live our daily lives the level of existence that we establish will be of our own making. To get the most out of life we should live as best we can in accordance with spiritual law, accepting responsibility for our actions and the consequences that follow. Behaviour in the physical life cannot be divorced from the spiritual legacy because they are interdependent. The more we are spiritually aware while in the physical state and the more we try to live in accordance with the will of God, the fewer problems we will have to face when the transition from human body to spirit form takes place.

In summary, the Sixth Principle is saying that every aspect of the life we lead, every thought we think, every word we say, every action we take, will have consequences not only for our earthly lives but also for our spiritual progress and development. In the eventual assessment that is made of the physical life we have led there will be no one to judge us and we will not judge ourselves. We will instead be given the opportunity to review what we have done, assimilate every aspect of our behaviour and decide what can be learned from a comprehensive survey of our lives. We will know that what has happened is in the past and cannot be changed, and although it cannot be changed, lessons can nevertheless be drawn.

This newly-acquired understanding can be used to ensure that we and others benefit when the results of our lessons are put to positive use. We shall then be able to move on, perhaps with a chance to help those to whom we caused distress or anguish, perhaps with the opportunity to share joy and happiness with those whose lives we enriched.

The Sixth Principle underlines the challenges to be faced both in this phase of life and in that which will follow. Challenge should not be feared but seen as opportunity, because in working for spiritual advancement we shall find ourselves sharing the companionship of loving and enlightened souls who will support and sustain us in our endeavours.

We are part of the Supreme Being, and God in His wisdom understands our frailties. We are not punished because we fail to understand His intentions, rather we are given further opportunities to amend, put right and try again in order to promote our eternal spiritual progression.

Seventh Principle

Eternal Progress Open to
Every Human Soul

Eternal Progress Open to Every Human Soul

The philosophy of Spiritualism is built on the Seven Principles. Previous chapters of this book have indicated that at the heart of these Principles is the concept that there is a Living Force, often termed God, Which has created all that exists and Which maintains all its creations in a balanced universe. There is nothing that exists which is not part of this Being and nothing can exist that has not been created by this Force.

We understand from the Seventh Principle that God does not ever turn His face away from us. We are His children and He loves us. He does not give up on us no matter what we have done or how little we have learned. This does not mean that God condones or approves of injurious behaviour or iniquitous actions, but rather that He is patient with us and with our failings and gives us the chance to redeem ourselves over time. The length of time it will take does not concern Him; what is of greater importance is that we are willing to take action to make improvement.

He will rejoice in the knowledge that we are prepared to look at ourselves, examine our past actions and accept responsibility for them. It will, of course, be our personal choice whether or not we seize the opportunity to further our spiritual development or remain where we are. We may think that the effort required to redeem our earthly transgressions is rather like a mountain to climb, but if we recognise the need to make reparation for any damage or hurt we have done, we can rest assured that support will be provided by those in the realms of spirit who will help us in this endeavour. In the timelessness of the spirit world the length of journey we make is immaterial; what is important is that we seek opportunities to repair, rectify and make good our errors and renew our efforts to do better for the sake of our spiritual progression.

The knowledge that we are important to God and will be given the opportunity to atone for our transgressions should be a spur to us all. From the highest to the lowest, the richest to the poorest, intellectual to uneducated, all are equal in the eyes of God and will one day arrive at the level of unfoldment befitting their progression. There is nothing daunting about aiming for perfection; it is only a goal to which all may aspire regardless of origin or opportunity.

The Seventh Principle assures us that we are able to achieve a purer and more refined spiritual state if we so desire. Eternal progress is ours if we choose to accept the challenge. God has provided for our benefit this immutable truth so that we may work towards the fulfilment of our true spiritual potential. We are never lost from the sight of God and He will always be there to pick us up when we fall and to soothe us when we have failed. Equally, He will rejoice with us when we have surmounted an obstacle or achieved a goal. His wish is only for our greater good and that we should enhance our spiritual selves and move onward.

It is our responsibility to accept that there is further progress to be made and work to be done in order to achieve greater spiritual evolution. We are given unlimited time in which to develop our spiritual potential and as we unfold we shall find ourselves sharing the companionship of those enlightened souls who have been charged with the task of assisting us on our way. As we journey onward with these spirit helpers we shall enter spheres of ever-increasing spiritual evolution and knowledge that will offer levels of joy and fulfilment as yet unknown to us. The level of progression of a soul is defined by the quality and brightness of its spiritual light and purity. As we address the spiritual work we wish to do and that which is assigned to us, we shall find ourselves moving among evolved souls of a higher spiritual nature. The more evolved the soul, the greater its light and purity, and this is the goal towards which we should work in order to fulfil our own spiritual potential.

The First Principle, The Fatherhood of God, as it has earlier been amplified, is the core and root of the entire philosophy of Spiritualism. Each of the following Principles expands an aspect of that initial understanding. Each Principle develops ideas inherent in, and completely dependent upon, those four seemingly simple words of the First Principle. There is no idea developed in the subsequent Principles that falls outside the all-embracing concept conveyed by those words. Further, it is evident that each of the subsequent Principles is linked not only to the first but to all the others.

The entirety of the Seven Principles has to be maintained as a whole – this is not a 'mix and match' philosophy. Whilst each

Principle can be studied and discussed individually, there is a need to come back to the wholeness of what they express in order truly to comprehend their meaning.

When considering the Seventh and final Principle we have to bear in mind what has been discussed earlier. We have established that there is a Supreme Being; that this Being is timeless and has always existed and will continue to exist for all time; that this Being is All Love and All Knowledge; that we have been created by and are an essential part of this Being, sharing its abilities and capabilities. We have established that each of us is an individualised spiritual being which for a time inhabits a physical body. This physical body is discarded at death and the inner part, the spirit or soul, continues after this process to live and to love.

It is acknowledged that this individualised spirit has far to travel on its journey to comprehend the true and total nature of that of which it is a part. Indeed, it is fair to say that the process of seeking deeper understanding will take such a length of time as to be beyond the bounds of human awareness or comprehension. A thousand years, or even a million years, is a short span in the evolution of our own planet, let alone of the universe as a whole. We hear and read of the evolution of life on this globe which we measure in terms that are virtually impossible to absorb, as all we have is the yardstick of our own individual life and the lives of those around us.

It is natural to question at what point progress is finished and perfection reached – indeed can perfection ever be reached? Here we need to be realistic and acknowledge that in spirit, as in physical life, we will never know the answer to all things and can only put forward our ideas of perfection. The finite cannot comprehend the infinite. One thing we can be sure of is that whatever God has in store for mankind in general and for each of us in particular, it will come to pass at some time in our evolutionary progress. We will all meet our Maker, however long it may take.

In using the word 'eternal' can we ever hope to grasp what 'eternal' means? The Ice Age or the Neolithic Age or any other Age seems an eternity to us when described as being many thousands of years in length. The Dark Ages or the Age of Reason or any one of the many Ages referred to in our history may have lasted merely tens or hundreds of years. We can only view or value things in terms that we have experienced or which we understand. We accept the concept of eternity either by faith or by reason and when we use the term 'eternal' we understand it as being time that never ends.

Each of the Principles asks us to use that which is known within our lives as the starting-point for a journey into the unknown. As human beings it is part of our nature to want to reach further than our arms can extend. It is because we are part of the ever-continuing expansion of the God-energy that we want to expand our personal nature. This is what is understood as progress. Studies of evolutionary development have shown change and progress running as central themes throughout the existence of life on Earth and through the history of mankind. There may have been periods when a minimal amount of progress has been made but, taking the long view, we can see that since man's first appearance there has been both physical and spiritual progress.

Recorded history and scientific study show that humanity has progressed in physical terms from a primitive organism to the ever-developing human being of today, who can not only walk upright but also master much of his environment and introduce technological innovation. Progress in the human evolutionary context needs to be viewed on a long-term basis. The less spiritually-developed aspects of man's nature have led him to wage war, to cause pain and suffering, to promote fear and distrust and to show many negative sides of his character. The higher self has shown positive aspects and led him to be loving, creative, artistic, inspired and inspirational.

Ultimately there is acceptance within all the Principles that the higher aspirations will triumph. As men are at widely differing levels of spiritual attainment, there will be, for the foreseeable future, those who will not want what is best for the whole of mankind, concentrating their efforts only on personal gain and satisfaction. Over time, each individual will come to understand that personal well-being and growth are not simply dependent on what one does for oneself. It is linked with what one does for others and is part of the unfoldment of the Divine Plan that Spiritualists accept exists for mankind, the world and creation as a whole.

Many people take exception to the fact that those who have lived other than exemplary lives will be able to progress in the same way as those who have lived good lives. What is good and bad is a matter of opinion. Who has the right to judge another when we are seldom conscious of the reasons for his actions? The perpetrator may well not have been aware of the consequences that could arise as a result of his actions. Should God pass judgement on an individual for his actions in life He would cease to be impartial. It is the impartiality of God which ensures that when we talk of Divine Justice we will not be measured against the standards of anyone but ourselves. As individuals, only we have the right to judge our thoughts, motives and actions when we are fully aware of the consequences.

Spiritual progression is open to all and it is for each person to choose when and in what manner and even in what surroundings to make progress. For some, a great deal of progress may have been made during their period of life on earth. For many others, there will have been more limited progress. For yet others there will have been little or no progress.

Each of us is now undergoing a life that is just a tiny proportion of the time in which we will exist in an individualised form. For those who already want to move forward continued progress will come easily. To those who are less accustomed to self-examination of motive and action future situations will only slowly bring an awareness of opportunity. For those who have chosen to stand still forward motion will be more difficult. There will always be opportunity, and certainly encouragement. Progress will always be open to those who decide to make that choice.

It is implicit from the use of the words 'open to' in the phraseology of this Principle that will or personal desire is the cornerstone of when and how progress is to be achieved. There has to be a deliberate and conscious decision to follow that which each of us adjudges to be good. It may be that, for some, making that conscious decision will take what in itself seems an eternity. However, there will come a time for every person when he or she realises that the moment has arrived to begin to make progress. We have made it clear that personal responsibility is of enormous importance. There is also an overriding requirement within the Plan of God for each person to become more aware of his own spiritual nature and of his spiritual relationship with all forms of life and with the Godhead itself.

For almost everyone the desire and need to progress will come to the fore within a relatively short period of time. Only for the most recalcitrant will there be the need for spirit helpers to make them face up to the reality of progress. Even then it will be done by reason and encouragement, with love being the motivational force behind their actions. The need to appear to be cruel to be kind will be a last resort – but firmness will always be the final option. No one can escape progression.

Progress will apply to all forms of life however they may manifest. We have already accepted that man has a particular and specific role to play in the advancement of the cause of truth, justice, wisdom and love. Other life-forms have different roles to play, not as actively demanding in this advancement but still of great importance as they enhance and support the efforts of man in his supreme task.

All that has been created by God – which means all that exists – is subject in some measure to the concept of progress simply because it is part of God. This poses an interesting question – if all that God has created will, in some way and at some time, progress, does this suggest that God Himself is subject to His own Laws and that progress applies not just to the individualised spirit but to the Great Spirit itself? There would seem to be a viable case to support an affirmative answer. The God of yesterday was sufficient for yesterday, the God of today is sufficient for today but the God of tomorrow will have to grow, progress, expand and develop to be sufficient for tomorrow. Tomorrow has not yet arrived, but when it does it will bring actions, reactions, experiences, knowledge and wisdom that have yet to be created. Perhaps, then, God also has to progress.

We have established Principles for God's creations. Can we then be bold enough to suggest that mankind has been touched by energies and forces which have indicated Eternal Laws that apply equally to God and His creations? Some will question our ability or right to make such suggestions, but if there is truth in the concept of progress, now may be the time for mankind to work with his Creator, not just as a creation or subject but as a member of the team or even partner – a very junior partner certainly, but nonetheless a partner.

The potential to develop God-given and God-like abilities lies within all of us. The challenge of the philosophy of Spiritualism as indicated in its Principles is to begin or expand our development, not to say that we are equal to God or to challenge God, but to work longer, harder and with greater enthusiasm to bring about the fulfilment of His plan for all that has been created. If this potential has been implanted in each of us, can we do other than answer the call?

The hope that is expressed for us in the wording of 'Eternal Progress Open to Every Human Soul' is shown in the love of God and His understanding of our needs. He knows that we are not perfect and that we have stumbled many times on our earthly pathway, but equally He knows that we have the ability to improve and make good the soul and spirit we are. His trust in us will never fail. Let our confidence in Him be foremost in our thoughts and in our lives. God shares so much with us and now is the time to respond.

Conclusion

The review of the Seven Principles set out in this book is an attempt by a small group of Spiritualists to put down in print their collective thoughts, having spent a great deal of time considering the Principles in the light of current understanding and modern terminology. This document should not be regarded as the authorised or definitive version of the Seven Principles. It does not seek to establish creed or dogma, nor does it call for unqualified acceptance. It does not decree how one should think or what opinion one should hold. The book offers ideas for discussion in the hope that they may suggest new or different avenues of exploration. Spiritualist readers will already be aware of the diversity of background, experience and understanding that exists within modern Spiritualism. Enquirers will perhaps begin to comprehend the extent of the diversity of opinion on Spiritualist philosophy.

In compiling this book the authors have spent much time studying the opinions and reasoning of many writers and commentators on spiritual matters, from the past to the present. In addition to the study time undertaken, the authors have had many hours of discussion and deliberation together. These have focused not only on concepts but also on the wording of the Seven Principles themselves. In-depth examination of the Principles has been of great value in establishing a clearer understanding of what the spirit inspirers and originators intended to convey.

The interpretation of the Principles has not been an easy exercise. Seemingly simple expressions have been found to have immense implications. What initially appeared to be a few well-chosen and easy-to-follow words turned out to be profound, encapsulating ideas of great magnitude which impinged upon every aspect of human life, both now and in the future. The philosophy built on the Seven Principles has taken on a new and challenging aspect as a result of this work. The authors are in agreement that the time and effort spent on research has been of enormous personal value. They feel that they now have a far greater understanding of what was meant when the Seven Principles were first laid down. It is impossible today to put oneself into the minds of the early Spiritualist pioneers and their spirit helpers, but the authors of this current work feel they have managed to capture some of the original intentions and ideas behind the words.

The explanation of the Principles contained within these pages is not intended to be the final and definitive version. It is expected that future generations of Spiritualists will, with their extended knowledge and understanding, discover further interpretations and explanations. The contents of this book are offered for discussion and reflection. It is hoped they will generate interest and stimulate further research so that the philosophy of Spiritualism does not stand still. Readers are asked to make their own assessments and reach their own conclusions, because the essence of Spiritualist philosophy is freedom of thought and free will.

The authors are grateful for the opportunity that has been presented to them in writing this book. It has been illuminating work. They feel they have gained a deeper personal understanding and awareness, and hopefully greater wisdom, having spent much time in individual examination and reflection prompted by the work in hand. There has of necessity also been exploration of views held for many years and a certain amount of clarity gained and adjustment made as the lessons contained in the philosophy have been absorbed. Each of the writers would like to think that he or she knows more now than when the task was embarked upon, but none has a feeling of knowing more than any other person. Everyone has their own personal spiritual journey to make and their own pathway to find.

Thanks are expressed for the ideas, support and help from previous members of the Philosophy and Ethics Committee. All members of the writing team are of the view that their individual and collective contributions have been supplemented by inspiration from those in the spirit world who return to assist all those who are seeking greater awareness and understanding. Without that inspiration this book would not have been produced.

Philosophy and Ethics Committee, 2007